Sequencing
Writing Activities

Grades 1-2

Written by
Phyllis Bass

Illustrated by
Leslie Franz

Copyright©1987 Frank Schaffer Publications, Inc.
All rights reserved—Printed in the U.S.A.
Published by **Frank Schaffer Publications, Inc.**
23740 Hawthorne Blvd.
Torrance, CA 90505

Good Morning

1. _______________________

2. _______________________

3. _______________________

1

Kitty's Dream

1.

2.

3.

Dinosaurs

- All the dinosaurs died.
- Dinosaurs hatched from eggs.
- They roamed the earth.

1.

2.

3.

Apple Time

Then Roy baked a pie.

He peeled and cut the apples.

Roy picked the apples.

1.

2.

3.

Name ___________________

Snowy Day Fun

- She made a funny snowman.
- Jenny went outside.
- She rolled a big snowball.

1. ___________________

2. ___________________

3. ___________________

     FS-8454   Sequencing Writing Activities

Bunny Goes Home

- He runs under a giraffe.
- Bunny jumps over a flower.
- Last he hops into his hole.

1. ___________________________

2. ___________________________

3. ___________________________

     FS-8454   Sequencing Writing Activities

Name ___________

A Weather Wish

1. _______________

2. _______________

3. _______________

 FS-8454 Sequencing Writing Activities

Eggs-plain This!

1. ____________________

2. ____________________

3. ____________________

4. ____________________

8

FS-8454   Sequencing Writing Activities

Name

Cross With Care

1.

2.

3.

4.

FS-8454   Sequencing Writing Activities

Write the sentences in order.

The Big Change

- I hatched from a tiny egg.
- Last I became a butterfly.
- I ate leaves and grew.
- Then I slept in a cocoon.

1.

2.

3.

4.

10

FS-8454   Sequencing Writing Activities

A Nutty Surprise

- Later I came back to eat them.
- I gathered nuts for the winter.
- Then I hid them in this pot.
- Nuts! My nuts have sprouted.

1. ___________________

2. ___________________

3. ___________________

4. ___________________

Spooky Fun

- Then knock on a door.
- Find a big bag.
- Wear a white sheet.
- Say "Trick or treat!"

1. ___________________________

2. ___________________________

3. ___________________________

4. ___________________________

FS-8454   Sequencing Writing Activities

Suit Up for Space

1.

2.

3.

4.

FS-8454   Sequencing Writing Activities

Write the
sentences
in order.

Start the Computer

Wash your hands.

Turn on the computer.

Put the disk
in the drive.

Hold the disk
by the label.

1.

2.

3.

4.

FS-8454   Sequencing Writing Activities

Feed a Bird

1. ____________________

2. ____________________

3. ____________________

Let's Bowl

- The ball hits the ten pins.
- Irma bowls after school.
- She rolls the ball down the lane.

1. _______________________

2. _______________________

3. _______________________

Lucy's Lesson

- Lucy fell off her bike.
- Lucy got a new bike.
- Mom took Lucy to the doctor.
- She rode it with no hands.

1. _______________________

2. _______________________

3. _______________________

4. _______________________

  FS-8454 Sequencing Writing Activities

Meet an Octopus

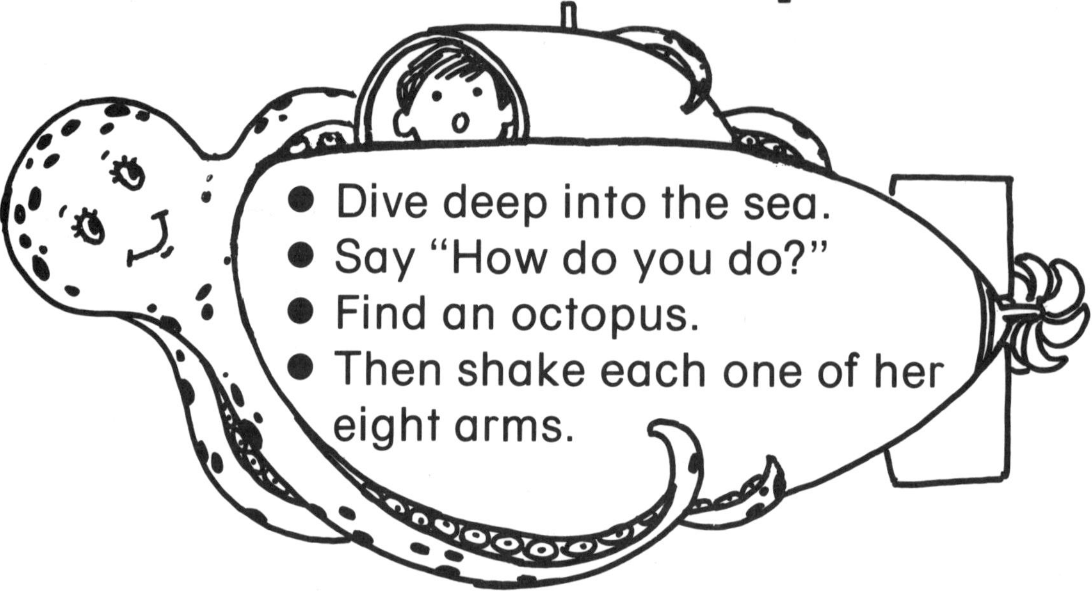

1. _______________________________

2. _______________________________

3. _______________________________

4. _______________________________

My Dog

- He barks at the waves.
- He likes the beach.
- Sandy is my dog.
- Then he rolls in the sand.
- It makes Sandy sandy!

1.

2.

3.

4.

5.

FS-8454   Sequencing Writing Activities

Name

Fingerpaint Recipe

- Mix I cup paste and I cup liquid soap.
- Make a picture with your hands.
- Add 6 drops of food coloring.
- Wet a piece of paper with water.
- Put some paint on the wet paper.

1.

2.

3.

4.

5.

Answers

Page One
1. The clock wakes up Glen.
2. Glen dresses himself.
3. Then he walks to school.

Page Two
1. I see a mouse.
2. The chase is on.
3. Now I have two treats.

Page Three
1. Dinosaurs hatched from eggs.
2. They roamed the earth.
3. All the dinosaurs died.

Page Four
1. Roy picked the apples.
2. He peeled and cut the apples.
3. Then Roy baked a pie.

Page Five
1. Jenny went outside.
2. She rolled a big snowball.
3. She made a funny snowman.

Page Six
1. Bunny jumps over a flower.
2. He runs under a giraffe.
3. Last he hops into his hole.

Page Seven
1. First it is a sunny day.
2. Next the sunshines goes away.
3. Then money falls from
   clouds of gray.

Page Eight
1. I lay eggs.
2. I sit on my eggs.
3. The eggs hatch in 21 days.
4. This is not my child!

Page Nine
1. Stop at the corner.
2. Look one way.
3. Then look the other way.
4. Cross when the street is clear.

Page Ten
1. I hatched from a tiny egg.
2. I ate leaves and grew.
3. Then I slept in a cocoon.
4. Last I became a butterfly.

Page Eleven
1. I gathered nuts for the winter.
2. Then I hid them in this pot.
3. Later I came back to eat them.
4. Nuts! My nuts have sprouted.

Page Twelve
1. Find a big bag.
2. Wear a white sheet.
3. Then knock on a door.
4. Say "Trick or treat!"

Page Thirteen
1. I put on special underwear.
2. I pull on the pants.
3. I must climb into the top.
4. My helmet goes on last.

Page Fourteen
1. Wash your hands.
2. Hold the disk by the label.
3. Put the disk in the drive.
4. Turn on the computer.

Page Fifteen
1. Stuff a pine cone with
   peanut butter.
2. Roll the pine cone in
   birdseeds.
3. Hang it in a tree.

Page Sixteen
1. Irma bowls after school.
2. She rolls the ball
   down the lane.
3. The ball hits the pins.

Page Seventeen
1. Lucy got a new bike.
2. She rode it with no hands.
3. Lucy fell off her bike.
4. Mom took Lucy to the doctor.

Page Eighteen
1. Dive deep into the sea.
2. Find an octopus.
3. Say "How do you do?"
4. Then shake each one of
   her eight arms.

Page Nineteen
1. Sandy is my dog.
2. He likes the beach.
3. He barks at the waves.
4. Then he rolls in the sand.
5. It makes Sandy sandy!

Page Twenty
1. Mix 1 cup paste and 1 cup
   liquid soap.
2. Add 6 drops of food
   coloring.
3. Wet a piece of paper
   with water.
4. Put some paint on the
   wet paper.
5. Make a picture with your hands.